The Genius of Tony Clark:
Seen In Hind Sight

Dr. Darlene Phillips Gaskins

DEDICATION

The work undertaken to bring this book to completion was executed with love in order to make things right, and move our families forward. It was written in honor of family, those who we are descended from: Clarke, Campbell, Castelow, Farmer, Gaskins, Gibbs, Hatcher, Heath, Ison, Parks, Phillips, Robinson, and Smith. Those that are undocumented, such as, Dodge, Delorean, Giglio, and Kennedy are honored.

CONTENTS

PREFACE

Tony Clarke, is Detroit's own legend. He may have been born in New York, but his career was made in Detroit, and almost erased in Detroit. Tony's heritage was hidden, and memories taken for reasons undisclosed. In spite of those obstacles, he was determined to leave a legacy, and he did. He was sometimes known as the "Madd Entertainer." His creative focus could bring to mind someone who has fallen down the rabbit hole. Often, over the years, he was referred to by his son, Geno Clarke Sr., as the "Jinx."

Have you ever been to Washington, D.C, and visited the statue of "Albert Einstein?" Were you to do so after reading Tony Clarke's story, you would better understand the reference to his life, as one that who has fallen down the rabbit hole. While researching Tony Clarke's story, I did visit "Einstein's" statue. During my research, I felt the need to visit Washington, D.C. around the fourth of July, Independence Day. While out sight-seeing, I found myself at the base of this huge statue. When I looked up at the statue, I recognized who the statue was. I stepped back and read the name plate. It was the statue of "Albert Einstein." Suddenly, all of the pieces of Tony's' life fell into place. Think of Tony Clarke as a young boy with humble beginnings from New York, with the talent, focus, and instincts of those with "royal" bloodlines.

Tony Clarke's story makes you think of genius and pathways. It also makes you think of G-men (government) and M-men, and I don't mean mama's boys, that M is for Military. Tony Clarke was a genuine music genius. He was the real McCoy. Be forewarned, the B word is used in this book: as B for believe. Tony Clarke's career, and demise continues to be the subject of various conspiracy theories, as the creed of the streets is upheld: You do not rat out your friends. Complete understanding of the knowledge that is revealed and shared in this work is equivalent to winning the lottery. You simply have to decide how to use what you have been given.

DARLENE PHILLIPS GASKINS

INTRODUCTION

A legend was lost in the summer of 1971. Tony Clarke, best known for his record, "The Entertainer," and appearances on the Dick Clark Show, was lost to us, because of domestic violence. Decades later, through the efforts of his one remaining son Mr. Geno Clarke Sr., and his daughter Toi Dionne Dawn Clarke, he is finally being recognized for the artist that he was. This book is a reflective biography with a focus on healing. The author practiced a little R& R, that is to, reflect and reveal, in order to present Tony Clarke's story. The reflections in this book paint a descriptive picture of Tony Clarke through reflective lenses. The journey covers periods from April 13, 1940, through August 28, 1971, August 30, 1971, through September 9, 1973, and November 23, 2012, and January 1, 2015, through January 31, 2016. It is an honor to bring to life an iconic legend. It is a privilege to be chosen, as a writer, and a matter of trust, as a cousin to the Clarkes, to present this book to the public.

DARLENE PHILLIPS GASKINS

ACKNOWLEDGMENTS

This book is a tribute of respect to Tony "The Entertainer" Clarke, an iconic legend. This book was possible through the collaboration of the cousins: Geno, Toi, and Darlene. Thank you, Geno and Toi, for your help and trust. The power of three accomplished this dream.

1 THE HOUSE OF CLARKE

Ghost Giglio——-and Thelma Williams (parents)

*

(Son) Ralph Thomas Williams (Tony Clarke) and —(wife) Joyce Elaine Heath

*

*

(Children)
Michael Angelo Clarke
Terry Anthony Clarke
Geno Clarke
Toi Dionne Dawn Clarke

Clarkes' Family Tree

2 **TONY CLARKE THE LEGEND**

Tony Clarke was born Ralph Thomas Williams to Ms. Thelma Williams and Mr. Giglio (Ghost). He was born in New York, and as a young boy, moved to Detroit, Michigan, the Motor City, with his mother, Thelma in 1950. Ms. Thelma came to the City of Detroit, as a single parent. Before the move to Detroit, it was as if Ralph Thomas Williams (Giglio), never existed. Tony's mother, Thelma married her first husband, Cyril Clarke, while Tony was still in grade school. Mr. Clarke had a military background, and he greatly impacted the shaping of young Ralph's character. Tony attended public school in West Detroit with his last noted attendance at Northwestern High School. It is known that he left school early, around the age of 16 sixteen, to begin his married life.

Tony's roots were begun in New York. He was later imported to Detroit, the Motor City. Therefore, his character was formed in the inner city of Detroit. Ralph may have changed his name to Tony and taken his step father's last name, of Clarke, but his DNA remained intact and lives on.

As a singer and song writer, he was home grown; that is, he was Detroit made. As a young man, Tony started out as an amateur singer/vocalist/performer. Tony Clarke was always known as a Sharpie. He was known as a nicely dressed, clean - cut, focused individual. The women in his past described him as having smooth light - caramel, latte - colored skin, with wavy to straight sandy-reddish - colored hair, and never a hair out of place. He was a little over six feet tall and packed with charisma. According to friends and family, he had a little swing to his step. He walked with a swagger. His was a well put together image that would stand the test of time, and betrayal. No, Morris Day of "The Time," and Prince did not create that swagger, or that stylish look with no hair out of place, and colorful suits. Tony Clarke was the original **styler.** Yes, he could whip that head around and flip his hair back in place while performing. His first recording was in 1960, on the Stepp label "Hot Rod Car." This started with him being taken under the wing of a mail man named Fred Brown. This venture into the music Industry, though not as successful as he had hoped for, motivated him to focus on a career in song writing, producing, and singing. Thus, began the roots of his family's motto, "Never, Ever, Settle," Something similar to Winston Churchill's saying, "Never Surrender." Though not much was ever said about Tony's biological father, Mr. Giglio, he had to have gotten that natural focus, that voice, and since of self - worth from him, the Ghost, as the Giglio name is a legendary Italian name. Ms. Thelma never talked about Tony's father, which led to speculation, about the Ghost in the Family tree, to include, from an undisclosed Chicago source, his being Sicilian. There are even whispers of witness protection to explain the sketchy picture of Tony Clarkes' beginnings.

According to his first cousin Saundra Howard, Tony came from that "Red Headed" Italian, a New Yorker, named Giglio. Tony's biological father may have been a red head, but all of Tony's sons were blonde. Tony actually expressed his feelings of not knowing his biological father in one of his songs, Ghetto Man (1969):

"When I was younger I felt A-shamed — Cause I never knew my Pap-A a's name — Then out of nowhere I found my pride— found a man don't have to hide." When you listen to "Ghetto Man," it makes your ears ring with Tony's "Key Signature," leaving you with an echo of the recording, Super Fly, playing over and over in your head. When you think of Tony Clarke, picture in your mind a young boy with humble beginnings from New York, growing up on the inner-city streets of Detroit, with the talent, skills, focus, and insight of those with royal bloodlines. Yes, his package of Talent was powerful, maybe too powerful for his time.

3 SECOND CHANCES

Tony's second attempt at song writing, hit pay dirt. Tony Clarke wrote "Pushover," something that he never was, for Ms. Etta James in 1963 with Billy Davis on the "Chess Records." The song made the honor roll of hits, and made the charts nationwide. Tony Clarke was on the road to being recognized globally! With Tony Clarke as the writer, and Ms. Etta James as the singer, another hit made its way to the public, in 1964. "Two Sides to Every Story," hit the charts. Tony toured with James Brown. He appeared on the Dick Clark Revue. He even got top billing at some of Detroit's well - known night spots like The Twenty Grande, Phelps Lounge, and the Rooster Tail. His recording of "A Wrong Man" in 1968, on the M-S Records will always hold a special place in our hearts, as he lived it and sang it from the heart.

This set the tone for a while with in Tony's career. He became the song writer, a true artist, writing for and working with some of the most distinguished artists in the industry, such as Danny Thomas, Aretha Franklin, David Ruffin, Wilson Pickett, and others. He was a success! Yet, this was not what made Tony happy.

Like most talented artists, he followed his heart and continued to pursue his dreams of hearing his songs recorded with his voice. This dream alone went against the current trend in the music industry. That is, he had the "Voice," not like others who needed technical enhancement or back up. Tony was writing about his real - life experiences, which allowed him to sing from the heart. He was as my uncle Leroy, his cousin, who spent a lot of time in Smokey Robinson's houses, would say a real crooner, and he could carry a tune and hit some high notes. Some of you are saying, "And how did you know that?"

I was my uncles' shadow as a young child; where they went, I went.

The following lyrics are reflections of Tony Clarkes' chosen pathway:

The Key,

Music and Lyrics noted to be by Tony Clarke and -Roger Spotts (1969)

Just dropped by to have a drink

Maybe even two

Bartender just a moment

I think I have a tip for you

I'll look in my pocket to see

What I can find

Oh, my do you see

This key was to my home

It opened my front door

But now the lock's been changed

I don't live there any more

My kids are probably playing with their toys

And by now my ex is in the kitchen

Telling them to stop the noise

Now I wish I were there to hear it

This key that I hold now

Only brings back memories of when we first bought our

house and how I used to rake the leaves

But somewhere along the way

Our love went wrong

Now we're apart and this key

Hurts me to my heart

Well I guess I better go

Before I start to cry

See you soon ol' Buddy

I'd better say good - bye

But before I leave

Would you please

Do a favor for me

Throw away this key

This one is a reflection, written in hindsight by Tony Clarke, found in his papers, dated, (1971), unpublished lyrics:

Why didn't you realize that you care

 Now at the moment of breakup

You decide we should make up

What about the times when I pleaded

Where were you

When I needed someone

To be by my side

You weren't there to change my stride

Didn't realized then that you cared

Why didn't you

Why didn't you realize

 then that you cared

I built my whole world around you

I blessed the day I found you

You treated me so unkind

I was the last thing on your mind

You never gave me any of your time

Didn't you realize then that you cared

Why didn't you

Now since I found someone else

And it's too late

Now I'm found

California Days and Nights

Lyrics noted to be by Tony Clarke, and Roger Spotts (1969):

The days were made for lying in the sun

Until your body's done

Then run out to the sea

The seas so cool and exciting to your skin

That it's a happen-in as the waves rush over you

California days Those California days

Strolling on the shore

Watching sea gulls soar is refreshing to the soul

A story to be told

One finds time to search the mind

The nights are made to hold the one you love

beneath the moon above

No better can be found

And as you kiss a feeling comes alive

And you're aware that this is where you'll stay until you die.

4 TONY CLARKE THE MAN

No, he did not walk on water. Yet, his songs could bring water. They still can bring tears to your eyes. He was a man, and he had faults. So, what was the legacy that Tony Clarke left behind in his wake? Were you to talk, and listen with his friends and associates, you would consistently hear the same theme: were you to listen. He was talented, focused, and persistent. He was direct, a straight shooter. Tony's legacy to his family was inner motivation, "Never, Ever, Just Settle." something Geno Clarke Sr., his heir, his son, has had to practice in order to re-open doors in his quest to set things right for his father.

Tony was known to be a sharp dresser. He was a smoothie, a wolf dressed in sheep's clothing. He was a natural in all things. Not only could he sing, he could write, and play the piano. Although he did not finish high school, he was a smart strategic thinker, which was validated with his hit "The Entertainer." When you study Tony's music sheets, and play his notes on the piano, you can see and feel that he saw patterns and could hear musical notes. It is as if, he liked to do jingles.

His Key signature" was **F- Major 7**. In hind sight, Tony Clarke came to the City of Detroit bearing gifts, and he was not appreciated. He was a light amongst some very dark characters. No, he was not a saint! His was a creative light, much like another Albert Einstein, only in the music industry. His friends in the industry will tell you that he did not know the business side when he started out. He was given a label and not much more, as far as recognition goes for his work in the music industry. Those that who really knew the man will tell you that he was a survivor, which should have given those business moguls in the music industry pause in some of their business practices.

He was also a pugilist. He was the self - appointed neighborhood watchman. This role was well noted in his community, known as Pilgrim Village. This old neighborhood was bordered by, Puritan Ave., and Livernois Ave., just shy of Highland Park.

He was the one you went to when family was wronged or physically attacked. According to his Sister - in - law, Sandy and cousin Saundra, he was a "Protector." According to one neighbor, Ms. Aimee, he was looked up to in the neighborhood. A legacy, he passed on to his sons. As a cousin, growing up in the inner city of Detroit with his sons, there was no fear. Just knowing that they could out box and win a fight with anyone, and had my back, I walked those streets with confidence.

Tony was also one of our infamous family members. No, he was not the "Detroit Hit Man." That would be an uncle. He did have an undercover role as an "Enforcer" for some heavy weights in the "Detroit Underworld:" this comes from a source who does not wish to be disclosed. Remember not to pass judgment, and keep in mind that he was, at one time, a struggling artist, and a man first, with a family to feed. Tony Clarke "Served" the Detroit community.

Tony was descended from the Giglio and Williams family. He married into the Heath family, who are descendants of the Farmer family. He married a grand-daughter of one of the "Three Sisters." He married Joyce Elaine Heath, — daughter of Rachel Heath Parks, Grand-daughter of Mamie Farmer (Parks), "great-grandniece" of Margaret Farmer (Campbell- Smith), and great - grandniece of Georgia Mae Farmer (Castelow). Tony had family, and he married into an even bigger family; One that was known to pass. They went out white to work and came home black. He was not alone in this world. He and Joyce Elaine had four children together: Michael Angelo Clarke, Terry Anthony Clarke, Geno Clarke, and Toi Dionne Dawn Clarke.

5 THE QUEST IN PURSUIT OF SUCCCESS

They called it his trip into "madness." Could this have been related to his desire not to be a puppet, though he wrote for others? Tony did spend some time locked up behind closed doors. According to his son, Geno Clarke Sr., one incident went something like this:

The family was at home one evening, at their house on Idaho. His dad, Tony and his mother, Joyce Elaine, were arguing, and his dad threatened to give away all of their furniture and the TV sets to the neighbors. As the argument continued, his dad actually carried out his threat and gave the furniture and Television sets to the neighbors. His behavior was strange, and progressed from there to violence. His mother, Joyce Elaine called the police and paramedics. When they arrived, his dad, Tony was so out of control that he had to be committed for his own safety. No, family members did not come to his rescue, as they felt he was where he needed to be. According to a close friend of Tony's; Tony called a friend, who just happened to be a lady, and shall remain anonymous. Thanks to this friend, Tony was released, and able to get back on the streets.

Thus, began his quest to succeed at all costs. He was a driven man. The undisclosed theory was that Tony had been slipped a Mickey, something that caused a chemical imbalance in his brain. It could have been PCP - laced marijuana or just straight up LSD in a drink. According to Mrs. David Ruffin, Tony did like to drink, and as smoking marijuana was and still is not legal, there was no admitting to that. The question still remains the same, Why, would someone want to cause harm to a rising star? Did they think of him as a "Hot Shot" or "Rogue" that needed to be reined in? If you listen to his song, "A Wronged Man," and open your mind, it will make you think about the possibilities, as Tony had a tendency to write about his real, - life experiences. Did he stumble on to a circle of greed? It was well - known that he made a point to stay far away from the "Motown crowd." Yet, the question has always been, did he stay far enough away from that crowd? The key to the riddle of who Tony Clarke was can be found in his music. Tony wanted to hear his lyrics and music sung and played throughout the nation. He wanted to hear real emotion in his recordings. He did not want to be robotic, according to a close friend, Charles Buddy Smith.

Remember when the lip - synch scandal came out with Milli Vanilli? Do you really think that was an isolated case, with all of the technology available? Tony Clarke was truly a genius, as there was a method to his madness. Just look at how thoroughly spread out his music is, and I don't just mean globally. You only have to listen locally to hear the signature of Tony Clarke. You can hear his **key signature**, or an inversion of it, once you listen. Take a look at TV and radio jingles and really listen. It will just make you laugh. Were you to listen to a couple of sound tracks from some early films, you might be surprised at whose **key signature** you hear. Tony knew what only another artist would know. That is, that an artist of any kind always has an individual signature. No matter how you copy or transpose the notes, the root note will remain the same. It will have the artists' design all over it. So as Tony felt that as long as he was alive, he would never get the recognition and status that he deserved. He strategically placed his music around others. Tony's music could be found written down on anything, such as brown paper bags, napkins, and scraps of paper. His written thoughts ranged from a few lyrics to full - blown compositions. Tony, knowing the nature of the people he was surrounded by, played the absent-minded artist who forgot to pick up and keep track of his written thoughts and work. Being an artist myself, it was easy for me to hear what my cousin Geno Sr. had already realized. When you listened to other artists' recordings that did not mention Tony Clarke as the song writer, you could hear his **key signature**; His sound in their work. Uncle Leroy, and Smokey would say, it's in the harmony, the balanced sound. No one is saying that these artists knowingly put their names on Tony's work. There are limitless possibilities as to how cousin Tony's work found its' way under someone else's name. Yes, there were those of you, who were given his music to work with, from someone you trusted. You should just consider it a "Gift."

Then, there were others with an agenda. Those who did just a little "cut and paste." At this late date, it is a moot point as to how they got their name on his unique signature. What is amazing is that they did not hear it, or didn't they? Do you remember, over the years, when you would see or hear about certain artists who no longer sang a certain song when they performed? They did realize that they had been misled, and they too up held the street creed of silence.

Tony really was a genius to be able to look ahead and see that his work would continue on, after his demise. You know, with all of the modern technology, it is a given that this would eventually come out, which probably accounts for all of the obstacles Geno Sr. faced with his first attempts to revive his father 's,

Tony Clarkes' music. There was guilt out there with the face of resistance, covering up years of

piracy. You could see and hear it with interview questions that were answered in the negative. For example: When a well - known singer's first spouse was asked, "Did Tony and your husband write and work on songs together?" The answer was, "No, they never worked and wrote any songs together in our homes." "Yet, they were in and out of each other's houses most evenings, and weekends, singing, according to Geno Sr. Tony was nobody's fool; why would you think that his son would be? So, Geno Sr. kept on looking into his father, Tony's music.

It seems that Tony's drive has evolved in his son, Geno Sr. These day, he demonstrates all that drive without any of the drama. For example, when I asked him to find the song, "Detroit," which was written by his dad, Tony Clarke for Joe Pep, Geno Sr. started his research. When Geno found out that Kid Rock had revived his dad's song, word for word, without saying Tony Clarke's name at the end of the song, and sang it publicly, in Detroit, during half time at a game, in November 23, 2012. There was no drama, only calmness.

Tony Clarke's children and family have woken up to the fact that without them, there would be no evidence that he ever existed. These lyrics by Tony Clarke were untitled and were found written on a letter head from his Toi Dionne Music Publishing Company at 15828 Idaho Street, in Detroit, Michigan. They were recovered after his death, in 1971. This is the original format/written in verse;

I don't know which way I'm gonna go

Should I go east,

No, I think I'll go West

but if I go West can it work out for the best

Or will people there look at us baby and

think our love a fright and

become up tight

I don't know which way I'm gonna go

to find a place where our love can grow

 a place where we can walk with pride

a place where we don't have to hide

6 TRUE LOVE AND JOYCE ELAINE

"My cousin loved him," said Pat. According to Joyce's cousin Patricia Ann Phillips (Campbell), she loved him. Joyce Elaine knew Tony Clarke or Ralph Thomas Williams, the man. She loved him with all of his faults. She was known to play their song "MacArthur's Park." My mother, Patricia, says that when she got the call that her cousin Joyce's husband, Tony had died, and she went around the corner to her house on Stansbury to support her, that Joyce just kept playing that song over and over and over; "MacArthur's Park." As my mother, took all three of her children with her to support cousin Joyce, I was there in that house where the tragedy was reported to have taken place. Being a very sensitive person, I can only recall a sense of peace in that house. There were no negative vibes or residuals of violence. The house was clean. I do recall always hearing music when cousin Joyce was home. My cousin Joyce let me show my support to her, by allowing me to come by and comb and style my cousin Toi's hair for school in the morning. This became the norm while we were all still at the same elementary school, Burns Elementary, in the inner city of Detroit. Geno, myself, and Toi walked to Burns Elementary School, together most mornings. Sometimes, my brothers would walk with us. My mother, Patricia remembers one of her cousin Joyce's goals was being able to attend nursing school. This is something I am happy to realize that we, her family members, have honored her memory by choosing health care careers ourselves.

We are a family with gifts, and Joyce could look at you and see "You;" that is, she could look into you and know your intent. My mother, cousin to Tony and Joyce, who retired from Banking, let us know that people of power do not like you near them when you see too much. Seeing people for who they are, is a part of our family legacy. Hence, the sabotage of a marriage or messenger. Yes, Tony and Joyce were estranged, with him commuting between California where he had established his own business, "Earthquake Productions," in 1966, with Roger Spotts as partner. You have to ask, was their break up by choice or by design? Geno Sr. says, "his dad thought that he was jinxed and/or cursed." Tony validated these thoughts and feelings when he sang "Love Must Be Taboo to Me." The following are a couple of unpublished songs written by Tony (1969) for Joyce and as far as family knows, never before disclosed to the public:

"Find Out"

Who's the fool

You or Me

We'll Find out one day

See if you can find a man

to be as good to you as me

Find out baby one day

We're gonna see

I bet you won't find a man who'll work

every day and bring you home

All his hard-earned pay

You think I'm your fool

You think I'm a square

One day baby you'll find out

here you had a man

"Old Father Time"

(Beach Beat-ATC-8140)

 Go away, but if you stray

 One day it's bound to catch you

 Have your fun

But when you're done

Watch out for Olde Father Time

Gone get you Darling

I cry, But it's your turn tomorrow

Leave me alone

But you'll run into someone

An unfinished work by Tony Clarke (1971):

Remember, Tony Clarke was an Aries, as it is reported that he was born in April. He demanded unconditional love, while enjoying absolute freedom. He was a man of the times. Yet, he married a woman who expected more. Tony wrote "A Woman of the Future," and he never did get around to writing the lyrics to that one. Joyce Elaine expected fidelity. What she did not expect was the betrayal not only from her husband but from those she considered as friend, and an industry that seemed to embrace Tony, while pushing her the wife away.

7 SPECIAL REFLECTIONS FROM FAMILY & AND FRIENDS

SAUNDRA HOWARD

Seen through the eyes of Tony's first cousin:

"Ralph was my first cousin. He was born in New York to Ms. Thelma Williams." His paternity is surrounded in mystery with whispers of witness protection and mafia. My instincts scream, "Government." "His father's given name was not disclosed. We only knew him by his last name of Giglio. Aunt Thelma later married Mr. Clarke. Aunt Thelma had several husbands, but Mr. Clarke seems to have made an impact on the young Ralph. When Tony changed his name, he took his step father, Cyril Clarke's last name."

"He came to Detroit as a young boy. He attended public school in the inner city of Detroit on the West side. Tony never did finish high school. He found himself about to become a father while in high school. They, him [Tony] and Joyce, were having Michael, and had to get married. Ralph married Joyce Elaine Heath in 1957. Ralph started his career in the entertainment industry at an early age in the late 1950's, as a singer and song writer. He drank and smoked, but I never saw him be mean to his wife. Aunt Thelma would tell me how he did not treat her as nice as he should, and I would tell him how he ought to not treat her so, as she was going to get him for it one day. I actually told him, "Ralph, that girl gone to kill you one day." "He wore hand-made suits, when he performed. His suits were made with love by the women in his family for his performances, which included the Dick Clark Show. They were gold, green, purple, and red. When we were growing up, Ralph was very protective of me. We were like brother and sister. He used to come over to my house and have jam sessions. Aunt Thelma's husband, didn't want them practicing at his house."

Special Reflections from

Geno Clarke Sr.

Tony's only living son, the youngest of three boys born to Tony and Joyce Elaine Clarke, is Geno Clarke Sr. He says, "that he was led to look beneath the surface regarding his father 's, Tony's career." Once you read through the unpublished writings left behind by Tony Clarke, and listen to his music, you too, will believe that Geno Sr. was, "guided by Tony Clarke, himself to look beneath the surface when the time was right to do so." Coming from a military and law-enforcement family back ground, it is very important to know the statute of limitations on certain crimes. Geno Sr. says, "my intent is not to cause harm, only to make things right for my father, Tony. So, know this, those of you who are still worried about things past, we are not looking in the direction where statutes of limitation do not run out." So, take a deep breath and open your mind. You might even do what Geno Sr. has recently found the need to do, — look toward "Jazz Music" and you may find what was lost or hidden. Now read the following unpublished lyrics by Tony Clarke (1971): (they were written in verse)

"I hear you say this is my country

and all that here is mine

But brother let me tell you

you just repeating that ole line

Sure, I know I live in the place

 but the streets ain't filled with gold

I worked hard for what I got

just to have it stole

and ain't got nothing free

I done most of the things."

Broken Trust (A Poem for Geno)

Lost a dad to tragedy

Never thought to lose mom so violently

Broken trust the root cause

Lust for power, money, possessions

Both brothers gone, one to motor vehicle homicide

The other to chemical and spiritual demise

Drugs, alcohol doesn't matter the cause

Wrong is wrong, and must be righted to further the cause

Of creating a legacy for generations to come

Police our own to right the wrong

Clarke, Heath, Campbell, Phillips, Parks,

Doesn't matter, wrong is wrong

When you police yourself, you learn to trust

Remember, family is **power**

Family Is not always blood

Broken trust can be healed with family and love

Listen at all times to the past

Not forgetting, just forgiving

Forgiveness is needed to move forward

To live safely in the present (Dr. Darlene Gaskins, 2017)

Identity Theft (A Poem for Tony)

Nothing new in the music industry

Just a different label

Young men and women erased

Through discrediting and forced addiction

Awareness breeds prevention and sometimes

Resolution, as family tends to not let the

Insult or injury go

Opening doors, resurrecting sunken ships

Some would rather leave closed and buried

Patience breeds success

Putting ghosts to rest (Dr. Darlene Gaskins (2017)

Special Reflections from

Toi Dionne Dawn Clarke

"As the baby and only girl born to Tony and Joyce Clarke, I got away with murder. I do remember him having a bad side. He used to fight, and grab my brother Michael. He would choke him up sometimes. I remember helping cook his dinners. He used to rent out the skating rinks for us. That would have been the one out on Schoolcraft. He was my "Daddy," and I loved him. My uncle Melvin Heath has always talked good about him, and how they would go out and beat up a guy who had hurt a family member."

"I remember when I was about 3 three or 4 four years old, I was outside with my brother Geno. There was this girl walking her dog, a shepherd. Geno started teasing the dog and the dog came at him and he pushed me in front of him. I remember my dad driving up in his pink midget/mini drop – top, and he went in the house and whipped Geno. Then he took me to the hospital."

"My dad is gone because of domestic violence. There is never an excuse or a reason for a man to put his hands on a woman. My cousin has a theory to help us heal. The theory is about why my dad became so violent at times. It involves chemical imbalances in the brain. No, these imbalances did not occur naturally. The agreed - upon thought is that my dad was in someone's way, and possibly a witness to a crime whose statute of limitations would never run out. It has even been said that he was "eighty-sixed." He was slipped a "'mickey." It was meant to incapacitate him permanently, mentally. He was also the victim of lies. What better way to throw a man off - balance and drive him to violence than by poisoning him with lies about his one true love, his wife? My dad was known as a lady's man. Yet, he always came home." We all know how vindictive a female can be when her attention and desire for a meaningful relationship is not returned on her terms. These days we just call them "pretty little liars."

Special Reflections from

Cassandra Williams

Sister - in - law Sandy, the youngest sister of Joyce Elaine Clarke. Sandy spent a lot of time around Tony Clarke. Sandy reflects back on the time when Tony and her sister, Joyce, lived in her mother Rachel's house.

"When they first got married, they moved into the house with mama. When Michael came along, Tony used take him and me to work with him. Tony was working in the clubs back then. Michael, my oldest nephew, his son, and I spent a lot of time back stage at The Twenty Grand in Detroit, while Tony and his peers performed. We had a back-stage pass. Most significantly, my recollection was that they always put us in a locked room while they did their thing. Those events are remembered, as the "'Back Stage Pass." My sister, Joyce, used to get so mad. She was not happy with Tony for keeping us, the kids, out so late, as we would not get home before 3 a.m. in the morning. There was one time, as a young girl growing up in Detroit, that a guy hurt me and my brother - in - law Tony took care of him. Tony looked out for me. He was a protector. He was always good around people. He was a father to my nephews and niece. Tony and my sister, Joyce, did not move out of momma's house, and on their own until after his career started to take take off. It is really memorable for me that Tony got my brother, Melvin Heath on to the Dick Clark Show to dance. This was very memorable, as people of color or blacks were not allowed on the Dick Clark Show to dance. That Tony arranged for my brother, Melvin, to dance on that show was really a great thing for him to do." Tony Clarke opened doors.

Special Reflections from

James Amos

According to Mr. Amos, he and Tony met around 1960 at The Twenty Grand. "We worked together at record hops. We even had our own place, that we played at when we finished at the other clubs. There was music, singing, and a little drinking, all at our place."

"There was a time that Tony wrote for David Ruffin, while he was at Chess Records, and that would have been when he wrote, "'Mr. Bus Driver Hurry." There were a couple of songs, that Tony wrote for himself, one of them was "'The Entertainer." Tony also wrote "'Push Over,'" for himself, which ended up being recorded by Etta James."

"There was an acting opportunity, where Tony had a bit part, as an extra in Sidney Poitiers' film "They Call Me Mr. Tibbs." There was this one incident that led to Tony's having to leave Detroit, and start up in California. It was a personal matter, an altercation on the inner-city streets of Detroit, that led to him leaving town. It was not business, and no one was looking for him behind the incident. Tony just felt it was the smart thing to do, and left town for a while. He geared up and headed to the City of Angels, California. Whatever the cause may have been that led to Tony's decision to head out to the City of Angels, California, it led to success for Tony as an independent label owner. Tony was not one to back down according to his friends," another legacy he left to his family.

They are still looking into what happened to Tony's business and work out in the City of Angels, California. There is a link to that mystery. Melvin Heath, Tony's brother - in - law, is that link. He was right there, acting as Tony Clarkes' driver while he was in the City of Angels. Cousin Melvin has not been available to talk.

Special Reflections from

Melvin Davis

Melvin Davis was a song writer and producer for Chess Records. He had ties to the Gordy family. His was a business and personal relationship with a female member of the Gordy family. Yet, he had close ties to Tony Clarke. So, think again when you say that Tony Clarke stayed well away from the Motown scene and label. Distancing the Motown net from Tony Clarke was near to impossible, as he and Melvin Davis worked closely during their time at Chess Records. When you ask any of the old - timers to think back and talk about Tony Clarke during the early 1960's through 1971, their reflections usually center around the "Money."

Whether they talk about how much he did and did not get paid for his music, how much his music is going for now, or who the "royalties" will continue to be paid out to, and who is entitled to the inheritance. The reflections are all about the "Money." Did you know that the royalties from Tony Clarke's music cannot be directly inherited by any other family member, besides his direct descendants, his documented and, recognized children without written declaration? This information should be useful in discouraging others from trying to put their hands in the cookie jar.

Special Reflections from

Charles "Buddy" Smith

Charles Buddy Smith can talk to you about Tony Clarke as a young man. He can walk you through the making of the record "The Entertainer."

"I can recall first meeting Tony, whom we called Ralph, when we were kids. Ralph, as we knew him as a boy, had moved from New York with his family to live in Detroit. Ralph had a different sound and style, as he did not start out in Detroit. When we were young boys, hanging out at my house, I remember liking his cousin, Saundra. We were around fifteen. I knew Joyce, who later became his wife, and her family long before Tony did."

As an artist, Buddy has given verification that Tony had a different sound, and that he had his own style. Tony Clarke's style was and still is so different that Buddy has asked permission to take three of his songs and reproduce and present them to the public in honor of Tony Clarke the legend.

Everything I Am, Love Power, and Hard Luck City.

Geno Sr., who is in charge of the business side of Tony Clarke's work now days, will work out the business side and distribution of royalties with Charles Buddy Smith. Charles Buddy Smith can tell you in vivid detail how things were for artists of color, during Tony Clarke's career. "You got passed over. You performed, but you weren't making any money, unless you got a gig with a white band. You know, Ralph just kept on doing his thing, in spite of the lack of recognition. I remember when he first used the name "Tall Tonio" for his song, "Hot Rod Car." He, — that is, Tony — had his own agenda. He was career focused. "Yes, I remember that Tony liked the ladies, but he still went home."

"Tony survived, while living in crazy times."

"Tony didn't hurt nobody." Charles Buddy Smith likes to toot his own horn.

When asked if Tony changed on him after becoming successful, Buddy responded adamantly, "No, there was no change in how we treated each other." For Charles Buddy Smith and Tony Clarke, it was a time of "Solid Social Lives." "You had friends," according to Charles Buddy. Just do the math and you will know the truth of what Charles Buddy Smith is saying, and listen to Tony's song "Land Slide." "It was Tony's final recording with Chess Records, and became extremely popular in British discotheques."

Special Reflections from

Yvonne Vernee Allen

Ms. Yvonne Vernee, who is still a member of the "Elgin's," went from High school, and talent shows into the recording business, where she met Tony Clarke. Ms. Vernee can tell you how well Tony Clarke's recording "Just Like You Did Me," has done in the United Kingdom (UK). She can even quote the going price for one of his original recordings were you to come by it, $4,000.00. She recalls, "Selling one for £ 3,000 pounds in the UK, not knowing at the time, the value. Now you could get $4,000 to $5,000."

Ms. Vernee can talk to you about Tony the artist. "I remember how Tony Clarke as a free-lance writer, not under contract, at Correct Tone in 1963, took me under his wing and taught me how to develop my singing style. While he was working with me, Tony would say, "'Come on, Yvonne give me that soul sound." Tony would also say, "'Put that in there for me Yvonne." "Tony was a good guy, "and he looked at me like I was a kid."

"I remember how, back then, me, and Tony worked on other songs, that never made it out of the studio. I remember how when things got rough, "They used a lot of records, that were kept in boxes to keep the studio warm, during hard times." Though he looked at me like I was a kid, Tony took the time to teach me how to sing. He gave me career tips. "Tony was very nice looking, and always neat. He, — that is, Tony — never had a hair or anything out of place. Now that is special, as Tony was known to be very focused about his appearance, while being absent minded about keeping track of his written work!"

Special Reflections from

Saundra Ruffin

(The First Mrs. David Ruffin)

Have you ever found that when you start asking questions of individuals and their activities during the sixties, that you find yourself trying to solve riddles? You have to remember, that to tell on anyone got you the label of being a "Rat." Talking with the ex- – Mrs. David Ruffin was like trying to crack a code for the government. Not only did you have to read between the lines, you had to listen between the words. She responded with an adamant "No" to most questions. Yet, she was eager to share the pending awards ceremony information, and previous award ceremonies. When asked if her, then - husband David Ruffin wrote and worked on songs together with Tony Clarke, she said "no." Her negative response was a surprise. Again, you had to pay attention, as the key word in her response of my question was "they," as she responded with, "No," they never wrote and worked on a song together." She did recall fond memories of Joyce Clarke spending time with her and her children. She recalls that, "Joyce had boys."

She never once mentioned Tony's good looks. Something all of the other women, that knew him or of him volunteered, without being asked. When asked to describe Tony, the ex- – Mrs. Ruffin's only response was, "He was a good guy——. We drank and sang, playing around at the house. They never wrote or worked on any songs together. There was a women's house in the neighborhood, where they hung out. It was a big house, always full of entertainers. It's a place to look into. People were in and out of there a lot. She used to book entertainers into the clubs. I lost touch with Joyce. It was a shock to hear how he, Tony, had died."

DARLENE PHILLIPS GASKINS

8 **THE TRAGIC DEATH OF A LEGEND**

Several accounts of Tony Clarke, a. k. a. Tall Tonio, are documented. Yet there are two eye-witness accounts that did not make the papers during that tragic time. At the time, they would have only been only children's tales. Tony's youngest son and daughter were there in the house on Stansbury Street, in the room where Tony was injured. Talk about PTSD (post -traumatic stress disorder), you know that they both have it. Other family members were there as well, and are now deceased: his mother, Thelma; wife, Joyce Elaine, sons, Michael Clarke, and Terry Clarke.

Geno Clarke Sr. was a 5th fifth grader at Burns Elementary in Northwest Detroit at the time of his father's death. According to Geno, his parents had a troubled marriage, [even] though they loved one another. Geno recalls seeing the paramedics arrive, and assisting his father up and carrying him out of the house. He remembers that the paramedics dropped his dad, Tony at one point and that his father was very much alive when he left his mother, Joyce Elaine's house on Stansbury, the night of August 28, 1971. Geno remembers hearing that his father, Tony Clarke had died at "Grace Hospital," and thinking that being dropped, after being shot did not help him.

Toi Dionne Dawn Clarke, his daughter, gives another perspective, a little closer to the heart of the matter, literally. She remembers biting the police officers' leg. She recalls standing at the door with her mom, and her dad breaking the window of the door at the top to get in, and her mom shooting at the top of the door and then the floor. She can remember there being a bullet hole in the floor, and then her dad getting got shot in the shoulder when he forced his way in. There was no kill shot. She recalls being down on the floor with her dad, hugging him and telling him to get up, and the police, two white officers, arrived and kicked Tony, her dad in the shoulder that he was shot in, while he was on the floor. She recalls telling the one police officer to "stop kicking my daddy, don't you see him trying to get up?" and then biting that same officer, as he continued to kick Tony, her dad. She remembers seeing her dad, loaded on to the stretcher, and taken to "Grace Saini Hospital." That was the last time that she saw her dad alive. The bullet wound was to in the left shoulder, according to Toi. (Reflection)All of the reported activity to the victim and wound area, by law officers, raises concerns: Tony Clarke did not survive.

Descriptive memories paint Tony Clarke as a victim. Could there have been foul play? Not just a victim of police violence, possibly of the music industry, and another victim of health care negligence? Possibly a victim of the music industry and of health care negligence? No wonder Geno Sr. refers to his dad as the "Jinx." As my mother, his cousin, Pat pointed out we have lost a few family members to a lack of care while in the Detroit health care system. So, which hospital system cared for Tony Clarke? Was it Grace Hospital? Did they have a policy in place of how to treat acutely ill and injured patients while in route to the hospital, and did it extend to people of color or perpetrators of domestic violence? Did the biases of public servants continue to be played out while in route to the hospital, resulting in Tony being DOA (dead on arrival)?

The possibilities of what actually took place that night, are limitless. Tony Clarke is known to be interned at the United Memorial Gardens Cemetery in Superior Township, Washtenaw County, Michigan. Yes, his family realizes that circumstances around you can influence your behavior. Yet, a higher calling can guide you around any obstacle to a better pathway. Let us end domestic violence. Changing one thing, can have a domino effect on outcomes, such as, never putting your hands on anyone in anger. Just imagine, if Tony had mastered that technique, my cousins might still have their father around.

9 GIVING UP THE GHOST

A legacy of inspiration, is what Tony Clarke has left behind. Following his multi-cultural success as a singer and song writer, his mark can be found throughout the music industry. You have to know that there was a method to Tony's genius, or as some would say, his madness. He strategically left a message to his family in his music, telling them how he had been wronged. We can talk about unearthing skeletons to bring clarity about to what Tony experienced at the hands of others in his short life. So, what are the odds of having a sister in the family who can give you a first-hand account, word for word, of what Tony Clarke went through with his music career. She can describe to you a moment of riding in your car, listening to the radio, and singing a song—and asking yourself how can it be that you know the words of that song, word for word? —— Having a moment of realization where you say, "Oh My God," that's mine—that's my song—How did they get it? — Thinking:

I thought I lost that notebook with my songs in it--. Having no words to describe the feelings of betrayal and violation when you realized that someone you trusted picked up your music and made it theirs—Yes, you know that you signed a contract, but you ask yourself, exactly what was in that fine print? — Yes, you are the proud owner of a record label—You now realize that you are theirs and what was yours is now theirs—Again, there are no words when you realize what they gave you, and that they did not even give you

"peanuts." Like Tony, this family member found herself, unable to prove anything, and was advised to let it go. She had no copies, and no proof, like Tony. So, like Tony, again, silence was maintained. According to another family member, they both found themselves on the carousel or merry - go - round. A circle of greed is what it brings to mind for me, with "lawyers" at the center of the hub.

Some people will say, "How did you get to that?" Some of you will choose to disagree with the interpretation. As a scholar, veteran, and doctor of education in leadership, some things you just know, and others you learn from experience. In short, armed with education, leadership, and ancestral spiritual guidance, success is a given. The main thing that you learn as a leader is how to listen. Tony's song "Just Like You Did Me," says it all.

This author has been there, as a government employee, working Medical Evaluation Boards out at Fort Hood. Only those who truly knew this author listened and believed! Tony did not have that family support back then.

So, he told no one what he had experienced at the hands of others. It is believed that the family guilt refused to allow the same thing to happen again to a family member. When my eyes are closed, Tony's presence can be felt. There are those in the family who will not hesitate to admit, that they can see Tony when they look at certain family members. What is truly amazing is when one of our children or grandchildren sings, you can hear the talent that lives on. Geno Sr. has believed for years that the Clarke family was hexed. Yet, he never considered that it may have been the Giglio branch that held the key to some of his family concerns.

What we, as a family, since Tony's tragic ending, have learned, since Tony's tragic ending is that a hex or curse can be lifted with love. Those who love, have trust, and faith in each other. You have to "Belicve," in order to succeed against all odds.

DARLENE PHILLIPS GASKINS

10 PICTURE GALLERY

TONY CLARKE

JOYCE ELAINE HEATH-CLARK

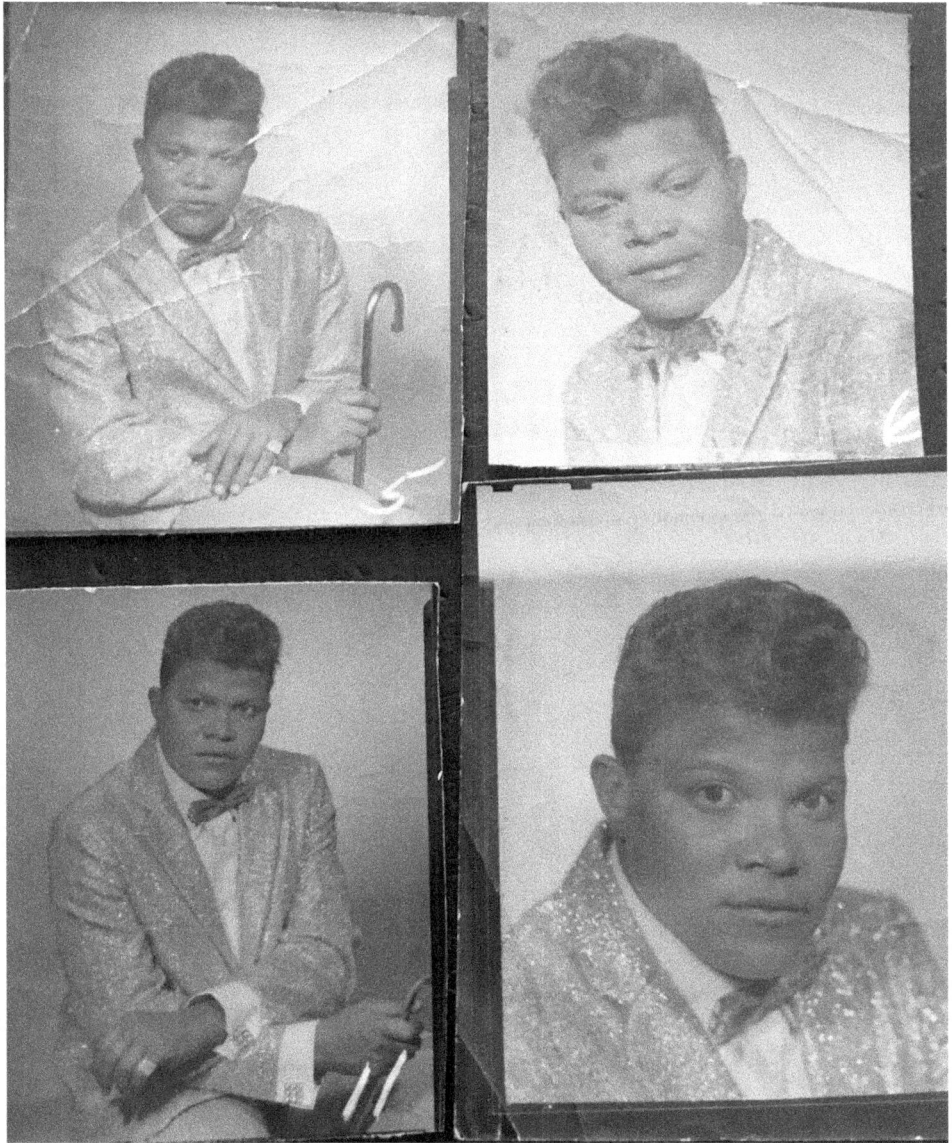

The Best Poses of TONY CLARKE

TONY CLARKE in California

A Copy of the Recording, The Entertainer

Unpublished Lyrics
on Brown Paper Bag,
as Tony was known
to leave around

TONY CLARKE a.k.a TALL TONIO

The Clarke Children, **MICHAEL**(back), **GENO, TOI,** and **TERRY**

GENO SR.

Father's Day Gala & Book Premier
6/19/16
Honoring
2015 Rhythm & Blues Hall of Famer
4pm til 8pm
Tony "The Entertainer" Clarke
Hosted by
Geno Clarke
DINNER & ENTERTAINMENT FEATURING
R&B Hall of Famer
Joe Pep & The Undisputed Truth
Hall of Famer
Special Guest
T.F.O Band
Mc Spyder Turner
Yvonne Vernee
Mack Rice
Contact info:
Geno Clarke (313)318-7409
Toi Clarke (313)808-5491
HTTPS://PayPal.Me/Fathersdaygala
[$50 Per Ticket]
St. John Conference Center of Southfield
22001 Northwestern hwy
Southfield, Mi 48075

Tony "The Entertainer" Clarke
First Annual Father's Day Gala & Book Premier
Entertainment featuring Joe Pep & The Undisputed Truth
Hosted by Geno Clarke
June 19th 2016
4:00pm-8:00pm
St. John's Banquet & Conference Center of Southfield
22001 Northwestern HWY, Southfield 48075
Facebook.com Tony "The Entertainer" Clarke
No. 095
First Annual Father's Day Gala & Book Premier
Entertainment featuring Joe Pep & The Undisputed Truth
Hosted by Geno Clarke
June 19th 2016
No. 095

Preserving the Legacy

Preserving the Legacy with a Legend

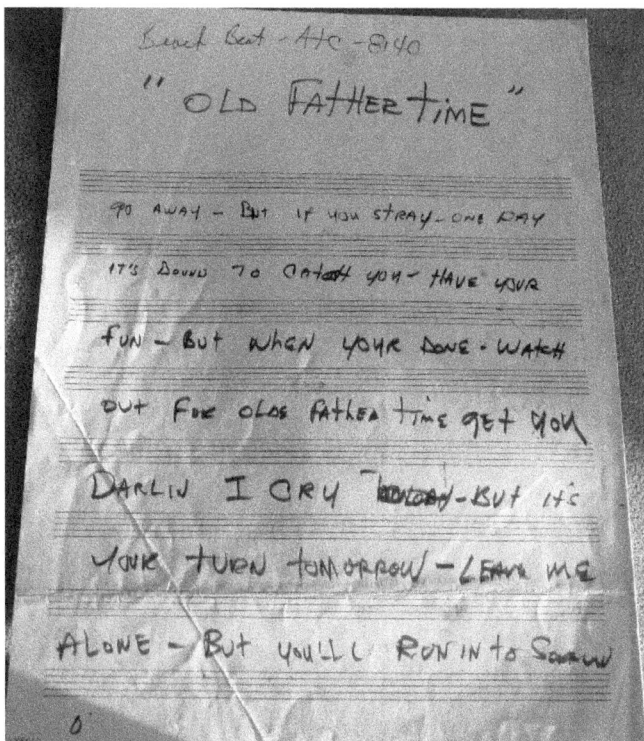

ONE OF TONYS' UNPUBLISHED LYRICS

Cousin to the Clarkes, DARLENE PHILLIPS 1978

GENO SR. at The 2015 Awards Ceremony

Cousin to the Clarkes,

TWINS, Cousins to the Clarkes

A Published Work of Tonys'

Remembering
TERRY CLARKE:

Grand Children of TONY CLARKE

Kansas City Cousins to the Clarkes, G2 & G3 (GREG)

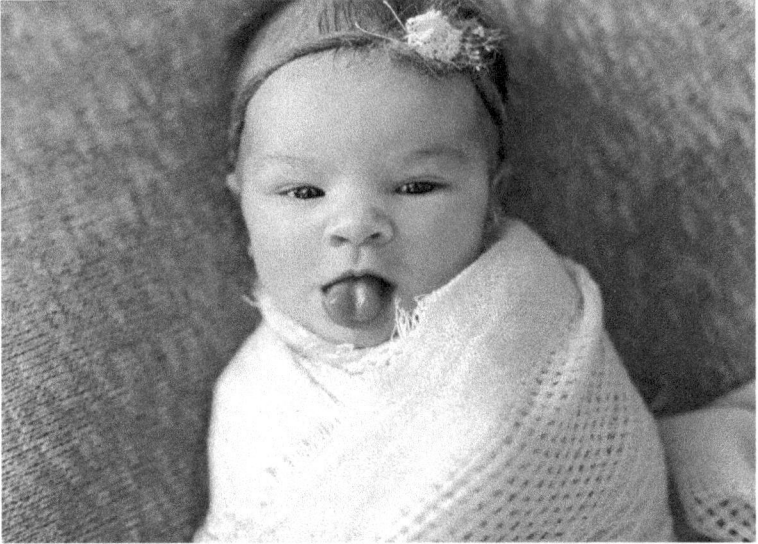

Cousin To The Clarkes,

MARGARET LUCILLE

Toidionne Music Publishing Company
15828 Idaho Street — Detroit, Mich. 48238 — Phone 273-6237

I don't know which way I'm gonna goe - should I goe east no - I think I goe west but if goe west can it work out for the best - oh will people there look at us baby and think our love a fight and become up-tight

I don't know which way I'm gonna goe - to find a place where our love can grow - a place where we can walk with pride a place where we do have to hide -

Unpublished Lyrics of TONY CLARKES'

Grandaughter of
TONY CLARKE,

RICKINDA

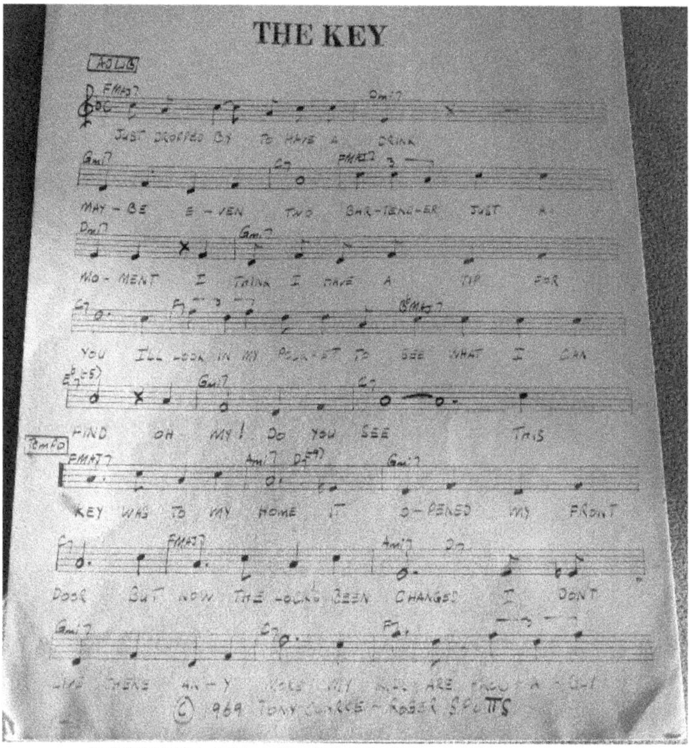

TONY CLARKES' Key Signature

The Remaining Clarke Children,
GENO SR. & TOI

Family: 3 Generations of Cousins

11 OPENING A DOOR

More than four decades, after Tony's death, Geno Clarke Sr., his son, got the "Call to Duty." He was chosen to see Tony Clarke's dreams prevail. It all started out very simple for Geno Sr. He recalls having a conversation with a painter, named Tony. Tony was painting Geno Sr.'s apartment, and they started talking about his dad and how he was a singer. It turns out that the painter's uncle was a D.J. (disk jockey) at a radio station. They talked and scheduled a show for early April 2015. Once they got together, things just started to move forward. Geno Jr., put the Birthday Celebration CD together of his grandfather Tony Clarke's recordings. According to Geno Sr., "it was as if he had a guide leading him to who and where he needed to be."

Geno Sr. found that even with a spiritual guide, he was still running into closed doors. So, he asked himself, "How do you get around closed doors?" He determined that you call in the next best thing to a hit man in the family. You call in the professional grade, that is a veteran. More to the point, you call in a peace-time DAA veteran (Detroit, Army, Administration Veteran). Geno Sr. called in his type A Plus, Plus, ++ personality, cousin. Geno called the foxhound, who also happened to be a scholar.

The journey of researching Tony Clarke puts you in mind of looking for a ghost, and I do not mean a spiritual one. It was as if someone had attempted to write Tony Clarke, a. k. a. Tony Giglio, out of history. Without the persistence of his family, we could have been calling Tony Clarke, "Legend Erased."

When listening to, and reading his music, you cannot help but see and admire his mental resilience. When you look beneath the surface of his work and the music industry, you will see that Tony Clarke was a model of success against all odds. When Geno Sr. started knocking on doors on his dad, Tony's behalf, all the old - timers could see was judgment time. They all had secrets to protect. So, what was a guy to do? He called in someone he knew that he could trust to open doors and preserve everyone's privacy, — his cousin, a leadership expert and author.

While his cousin did some research and interviewed, Geno Sr. did as he was guided to do. He continued to present Tony Clarke's accomplishments to the public. He began with the televised radio salute on April 13, 2015, to Tony Clarke the "Birthday Celebration." He did a live television interview with Billy Jones on June 10, 2015, on the Get Up, Stand Up show of Minister Malik Shabazz. He followed that with another televised interview on July 28, 2015, with Minister Malik Shabazz. On August 26, 2015, Geno Sr. shared his television time with Mr. Charles Buddy Smith and Mrs. Yvonne Vernee, on the Get Up, Stand Up show of Minister Malik Shabazz. The interviews were conducted by, Billy Jones.

Geno Sr. ended the year with a live televised broadcast on the Brenda Perryman 's show, "Table Talk on," November 13, 2015. During all of his social exchanges, Geno Sr. now found himself being referred to as Tony! Hearing his dad's name, let him know, that when people looked at him, they were able to see his spiritual guide. He knew that his dad was with him. Geno Sr. knew that he was on the right pathway.

The following are another set of unpublished, and untitled lyrics found written on small brown paper bags, as Tony Clarke (1971), was known to do: Please note the authenticity of the work, as there are some words that look like misspellings, but they may be part of the idiosyncrasy of the songwriter.

Now you know a plane can crash

A steak is so delicious but soon it turns into trash

You can always find a bargain

and it sure to wear out

and you can think swiftly

you choose but the one thing

I can't afford to lose is cash money

Friendship is friendship but that's been known to end

A baby's born sinless then he learns to sin

A ship will sail on water but now and then they sink

A fool is a fool but sometimes he thinks

And you can say anything that you choose

But there's just one thing I can't afford to lose

Is Cash Money

Say what you want, think what you will Cash Money

I hear folks talk about black or white and which is right

And some people think love's the thing

and feel it's out of sight

So, some good will conquer evil and someday it may

But when it comes to where I'm at

Give me my pay

I need cash money

12 Recognition of an Icon
Just Rewards

Tony Clarke (Ralph Thomas Williams) left us through tragic events in the summer of 1971. Decades later, through the efforts of his one remaining son, Mr. Geno Clarke Sr., and his daughter Toi Dionne Dawn Clarke, he is finally being recognized for the artist that he was. On Oct 4, 2015, Tony Clarke was inducted into the Rhythm and Blues Music Hall of Fame, in Detroit, Michigan. The event took place at the Charles H. Wright Museum of African - American History. Tony Clarke was inducted along with other deserving individuals, such as Aretha Franklin, and Ray Charles. He was represented by his son Geno Clarke, Sr. (No Change) and daughter Toi Dionne Dawn Clarke who sat in the audience surrounded by some very interesting people. For example, Tommy Hearns, the boxer, was sitting right in front of Geno Sr.

According to Mr. Geno Clarke Sr., the event went something like this: "My first red carpet walk was a little chaotic, as events were under someone else's control.

The arrival of the limousines was not as timely as they should have been, and other family members could not enter until the arrival of the inductees. Once inside, there was limited seating. It was as if the founder had sold twice as many tickets to this event: more than there were seats. I was excited to be here and did not worry, as I had a seat; that is, until I got up to stand in the line with the rest of the inductees. It did give me something to think about for future events. It was late when I was finally called to accept the award for my father. The inductees before me, had performed for 10 ten or more minutes after accepting their awards. So, I knew, that I had plenty of time to give my speech of acceptance.

"I proceeded to give my speech, of 4 four minutes, consisting of only two2 paragraphs. I found myself being rudely interrupted with negative comments about my family, — those that were no longer with us, — that I was paying tribute to. I felt, rushed at this point, and it made me angry. After I had waited patiently for hours to have my turn, here I was speaking and giving recognition to my family, and one of the hosts was rudely trying to cut me short. The guy actually said, "Well, damn, is the whole Clarke family dead?" I knew then that I was not dealing with a class act. It was insulting and rude. My sister, Toi, says that I turned so very red. I did the right thing, though, as we do not do witnesses in this family. I continued on and finished my speech. My dad was now officially in the Rhythm and Blues Music Hall of Fame. I had been here since 3 o'clock p. m. and did not leave until after midnight. I left that stage feeling victorious, as we had accomplished the goal of getting my dad, Tony Clarke, publicly and officially recognized. We had his award in our possession.

"I did walk and talk that evening with the inductees and celebrities. I took a picture with Dennis Edwards, now 71 seventy-one years old, who sung "Poppa Was a Rolling Stone." I took a picture with "The Fantastic Four." I said to myself, "I know this is only the beginning." This night, this event was a game changer for our family. We were no longer just survivors. We were now victors. I was even approached by a talk show hostess, Ms. Brenda Perryman, to appear on her show, "Table Talk," next month, in November 2015. I planned to be there, dressed as sharp as my dad would have been."

And then there is Toi Dionne Dawn Clarke, the youngest Clarke child, and only daughter of Tony Clarke and Joyce Elaine Clarke. "It felt excited to be there. I expected a more formal setting. We actually sat in an auditorium in kiddie-like chairs with our knees up in our chests. There were people everywhere, and a lot of them were sitting on stairs. There was not enough seating for everyone. I saw awards being given out to each member of a group and one award given to single individuals. There were people with $75 tickets. As the daughter of an inductee, my ticket was given to me, while my spouse had to purchase a ticket. There was no one on the doors taking the tickets. So much for accountability and business.

"Although I arrived in a limousine, I did have to stand up, outside for 2 two hours until the inductees were allowed in. The cars were late to pick them up. This contributed to the standing time. People were sitting on concrete steps; The place was over booked.

The entertainment, the singers or inductees were good. The inductees were asked to stand up behind those receiving the award, and were standing from 7 o'clock p. m. until 12 o'clock midnight. I stepped outside for a moment and came back in to hear my brother, Geno Sr., accepting the award for Daddy. He was saying that we needed to put an end to domestic violence. He was introducing the family in the audience, myself, and others. Then when he started to pay tribute to those who had passed away: —my mother, and brothers Terry and Michael, — they tried to rush him. The guy in charge said something like," 'Well, damn, why don't you say hello to all the Clarkes and pay tribute to them?'

"There was a book being sold with biographies on each inductee. It dishonored my dad, as it gave details of his death, while it only gave career highlights on the other inductees, as if his tragic death was the highlight of his career. It was unprofessional and hurtful. It could have simply given his career highlights and said, "'A legend was lost in the summer of 1971." I know that we accomplished our goal and got what we needed out of the experience —, "Daddy inducted into the Rhythm and Blues Music Hall of Fame." The highlight of the night was the "Award" itself. They had Daddy's picture in the background, and played his music while my brother, Geno, accepted Daddy's award. I was one proud daughter of Tony Clarke.

13 Saying Good – Bye

You may ask, how can someone write about Tony Clarke in such an intimate manner? It's not a mystery. It's all about hind sight, family, and love. Love is the key, believed to open the gate, giving access to mystical guidance. Being part of a gifted family, and one with love, anything is possible. Tony loved family, and that keeps him bound to "Earth,", allowing him to always be linked to a family member. As I said before, "Tony Clarke was no fool, nor was he a puppet. He was an original. He was "special," and he had "Foresight." So, it only makes sense to use hindsight to tell his story.

 For those of you who either stole and or sold some of his music, "just know," that, having access to his music was part of his strategy to have his music heard and remembered. For those of you who found yourself in the position of having unknowingly recorded his music as yours, because someone you trusted gave it to you, "no worries," as that was part of Tony's strategy too. He wanted to have his music heard, as he said himself in his recording "Land Slide," "I may not get my fair share but maybe the world will." He knew that he could not achieve his goals in the time that he had. He knew that you were in a position to get his music and jingles out there in front of the public, were he to find a way to get his music and jingles to you. You need to get past the guilt and forgive yourselves and move on, and **know that Tony has forgiven you.**

Thanks to his son, Geno Clarke Sr., and daughter Toi Dionne Dawn Clarke, the legend lives on. In life, Tony Clarke gave us **hope.** In death, he brings us **inspiration**, as his success has been uncovered, and hopefully no harm has been done. Though he was wronged, as he sings about in his record, "A Wronged Man," he upheld the street creed. He kept his silence and remained loyal to the end.

The following unpublished lyrics by Tony Clarke (1971) will make you think and look beneath the surface:

The Mystery of Life

The thought slowly revolves in your head

Why I'm black, you're white,

Your Pap is red

The answer' s not ours to know

Why a fellow is yellow has made you lay awake in your bed

The thing he tried to do was see if we could live together

You like strawberry

Myself I prefer peach

For that you won't hate me cause of my speech

All things should not be known and the wind may hold the

"key"

Let, they be the mystery

Do you know why

Why pretty flowers are born with thorns

 Why daytime makes you feel bright

And nighttime makes you blue

All things shall not be known

And the wind holds the key to life's mystery

And for what a man prays, often takes him away

But stop and think did you help a man become

A prey, for the devils within each man's soul

 Did you let him out to play?

14 This One Is for Tony Clarke

Geno Clarke Sr. (Geno, 2015)

"Dad, though people have been calling me, Tony, since I started this quest, I realized that you cannot replace a legend—. Your soul is one with mine—, and I know that you have been guiding me. — Since your death, it has felt as though there is a hex or a curse on the Clarke family, and due to God 's grace and the love of my mother, I'm lifting this jinx off of my shoulders in the name of Jesus—. I would like to say to you, Dad, RIP (rest in peace)."

This One Is for Tony Clarke

Toi Dionne Dawn Clarke

(Toi, 2015).

"All the years of having you, dad, were not nearly enough; but the memory, and legacy of you, shall live on forever through your grandchildren, great - grandchildren, and so on. Your music shall live on forever. My heart is still empty without you, but the determination to keep moving forward has been passed on to us. Proud daughter of Tony Clarke, Toi Dionne Dawn."

This One Is for Tony Clarke

Dr. Darlene Phillips Gaskins

(Darlene,2015)

"Remember me, Tony Clarke, as a link to the past——, a bridge to the future——, the entertainer for all times who shed no tears in public——. Know that I did it all for family—— I loved my family, and still do——. You can feel his love all around you as you write about him——. Tony, I know that you saw yourself in "The Tears of a Clown." –I know that you are still smiling. You are now more than a survivor. You are a victor. Most importantly, you are a Giglio, and a legend. I have nothing but love for you, cousin. Please know that the ghosts have been decoded. You will live on in our hearts. I hope, and pray that this work makes it right for you.

THE GENIUS OF TONY CLARKE: SEEN IN HINDSIGHT

His family

is his legacy

And

He lives

"The Entertainer"

Lyrics by Tony Clarke (1965)

You're the entertainer

The entertainer

You're the entertainer

The entertainer

You made' em laugh

And you left' em feeling glad

You made' em cry

And you left' em feeling sad

They've seen you perform

In so many plays

But they're not to know

You're unhappy today

So, they'll never know

Go on with the show

Cause you're the entertainer

The entertainer

You're the entertainer

The entertainer

The curtain's up and

Your audience is waiting out there

Now walk on stage, boy

Like you don't have a care

And don't let' em know

That you're feeling so low

Since your girl put you down

You're a sad - hearted clown

But the show must go on

Go on and on

Cause you're the entertainer

The entertainer

Now hear that applause

Now you know you made the grade

You fooled them well

For the money, they paid

Now walk off in style

And don't forget to smile

Though your heart tells you frown

You can't let the people down

Sure, your one girl has gone

But you've got to walk on

When you're the entertainer

Tell yourself

You're the entertainer

You know you can do it

You're the entertainer

Walk on in style now

 You're the entertainer

Come on, in style no

You're the entertainer

ACKNOWLEDGEMENT OF THANKS

Acknowledgments of thanks go out to those of you who were gracious enough to share your time and memories. Thank you for giving permission for written material to complete this book. Please bring to our attention, any errors or omissions. We will see that corrections are made in future editions.

APPENDIX

Music Compositions by Tony Clarke:

"Ain't Love Good Ain't Love Proud"

"Am I Losing You"

"Baby Baby Baby"

"Baby Baby Baby You're My Heart"

"Baby I'm The One"

"Before I Give My Love"

"Come Let's Do the Breakdown"

"Coming Back Strong"

"Crush"

"Detroit, Michigan"

"Do You Love Me Like You Say You Do"

"Don't Forget Me"

"Dr. Feel Good"

"Entertainer"

"Fugitive Kind"

"Ghetto Man"

"Guy Who Made Her a Star"

"Hey Senorita"

"I Wonder Now"

"I'll Make You Forget Him"

"In Time"

"Joyce Elaine"

"Just Like You Did Me"

"Landslide"

"Little Piece of Leather"

"Made of Honor Score"

"May the Best Man Win"

"Miss Loneliness"

"Mr. Bus Driver Hurry"

"No Conception No Sense of Dire"

"Poor Boy"

"Something Like A Storm"

"Storm In My Heart"

"Story of Woman Love And A Man"

"They Call Me A Wrong Man"

"This Heart of Mine"

"When You Lose the One You Love"

"You Get What You Deserve"

"You Gotta Choose"

"You Made Me A VIP"

"You're A Star"

"Pushover"

"Two Sides to Every Story"

REFERENCES

Amos, James, in discussion with the author Interview, Detroit Michigan, August 16, 2015.

Clarke, Geno Sr., in discussion with author, Interview, Detroit Michigan, (09/ 22 / September 22, 20 15).

Clarke, Geno Sr. Live Interviews. April 13, 2015, (Birthday Celebration, WCXI AM1160 Phenton Radio, with David Washington), (June 10, 2015) July 10(28), 2015, (August 26, 2015,) (Get Up Stand Up Show, with Bobby Jones) October 30, 2015, November 13, 2015(Table Talk, with Brenda Perryman).

Clarke, Toi Dionne Dawn, Interview in discussion with the author interview, Detroit Michigan, November 15, 201511/15/15.

Davis, Melvin, in discussion with the author Interview, Detroit Michigan, August 29, 2015.

Davis, Billy, in discussion with the author Interview, Detroit Michigan, September 6, 2015.

Howard, Sandra, in discussion with the author Interview, Detroit Michigan, August 09, 2015.

Phillips, Patricia Ann, in discussion with the author Interview, Detroit Michigan, August 16, 2015.

Ruffin, Sandra, in discussion with the author Interview, Detroit Michigan, August 23, 2015.

Smith, Charles Buddy, in discussion with the author Interview: Detroit Michigan, August 09, 22015.

Tabia, Aimina (Gloria Thompson), in discussion with the author Interview, Detroit Michigan, August 26, 2015.

Vernee, Yvonne (Allen), in discussion with the author Interview, Detroit Michigan, August 08, 2015).

Williams, Casandra, in discussion with the author Interview, Detroit Michigan, August 16, 2015.

Find A Grave. (2009). "Memorial #32966190," Superior Michigan, Washtenaw County, United Memorial Gardens.

Ancestry Archives. (Nov. 25, 2015). "Vital Records." www.ancestry.com November 25.

Newspaper Archives. (Nov.25,2015). www.newspaper.com. November 25.

Milstein-Spectroppop, Phil., 2015. "The Guy Who Wrote I'd Like to Buy the World a Coke Jingle Is from Detroit" Detroit Metro Times, archives (May, 18. Accessed2015/05/18). (Phil Milstein-Spectroppop) The Guy Who Wrote I'd Like To buy the World a Coke "jingle is from Detroit, November 27, 201511/27/15.

Lyrics Mode. 2015. Tony Clarke— "The Entertainer." lyrics, November 7. lyricsmode.com (11/7/2015).

Baranovichi, D. (2010). Voodoo o Histories: The Role of the Conspiracy Theory in Shaping Modern History. New York: Penguin Penguin Books, New York, NY.

Carrol, L. and& N. Cook, N. (2009). Alice in Zombieland. Sourcebooks, Inc. Naperville, Il: Sourcebooks, Inc.

Leonard, H. (n. d.). A Charlie Brown Christmas -Beginning Piano Solo. Hal-Leonard Corporation, Milwaukee, Wi.: Hal-Leonard Corporation.

May, N. & and C. Willis, C. (2003). We Are the People: Voices From the Other Side. Thunders Mouth Express, New York, NY.: Thunders Mouth Express.

Meyer, J. (2008). Never Give Up! Faith Words. Hachette Book Group USA, New York, NY.: Hachette Book Group USA.

McCullum, Brian. 2012. "Kid Rock Detroit Song." Detroit Free Press, November 23, .2012, Section A, p.1- – 2.

Payne, R. (2008). Simply Piano. Hinkler Books, Heatherton Victoria, Australia: Hinkler Books. pp. 20- – 23, 46, 59, 64- – 65.

Sandel, M.J. (2009). Justice: What's The Right Thing To Do? Farrar, Straus and Giroux, New York: Farrar, Straus and Giroux.

Winston Churchill Winston. Young Student Learning Library, (1991), 8th ed., 5:549.

Durham, Ernie. (March 13, 1970). "New sound tips, Top DJ's Choices of Records of the Week," p. 2. Detroit Free Press Archives. March 13. Accessed (November. 25, 2015). www.pqasb.pqarchiever.com.

Garrett, Cathy M. Office of the County Clerk, (1/4/2016). Wayne County, Michigan. (No, data) resource: Death Certificate.

Holiday, Barbara. (August 12, 1965). "Our Jazz Festival, Our Fair Festiva," p. 5. Detroit Free Press Archives. August 12. Accessed (November 25, 2015). www.pqasb.pqarchiever.com.

Rylatt., Keith. (July 26, 2011). "Tony Clarke – They Call Him A Wrong Man," Groovesville, USA (blog)., (April 15, 2015)., www.groovesvilleusa.com/blog/?p=919.

Old School Music Lover, 2015. N.A. (October 10, 2007). "Pushover" Last modified October 10, 2007. performed by Etta James (1963). Old School Music Lover. (April 15, 2015). www.oldschoolmusiclover.com

ABOUT THE AUTHOR

Darlene Gaskins is a Regular Army Veteran, married to a retired Disabled Veteran, and a mother of four. She grew up on the streets of Detroit's Northwest side. She graduated from Cass Technical High School in Detroit, Michigan. She is a Registered Nurse, a healer since 1983; graduated from Baker University with a Masters in Management (MBA without all the stats). She has been a stained glass crafter since 2003. Dr. Gaskins obtained an Educational Doctorate in Leadership to help make the world right. She resides in the Midwest, Kansas with her family, and returns home to Detroit frequently.♫

Other titles by Darlene Phillips Gaskins

Unlocking God's Gift to Me, the Mother-in-Law

ISBN: 9781682702369

The Author, DR. DARLENE PHILLIPS GASKINS

PERMISSIONS

Darlene Gaskins is authorized, by Geno Clarke Sr. to use and provide the Publisher, with access to any submitted materials pertaining to Tony Clarke. This release covers all materials submitted to the publisher to include photographs, music, lyrics, CDs, written copy or material from the Joyce Elaine Clarke estate with the sole purpose of publishing and marketing the book, "The Genius of Tony Clarke, Seen in Hindsight."

www.ingramcontent.com/pod-product-compliance
Lightning Source LLC
Chambersburg PA
CBHW071150090426
42736CB00012B/2290